From the Top

Written by Simon Mugford

Collins

From the top of a windmill in Holland, you can spot ...

a house by the canal.

From the top of The Shard, you can see ...

rooftops, blocks of flats and a long river.

From the top of this tower in Paris ...

6

you can step down to roads, boats and gardens.

From the Grand Canyon, you can see ...

red cliffs and a river.

From this balloon trip in Kenya,
you can spot...

big cats that sprint in the dust.

From high up in Hong Kong,
you can see ...

specks of light from the flats and night markets.

From the top

After reading

Letters and Sounds: Phase 4

Word count: 95

Focus on adjacent consonants with short vowel phonemes, e.g. /s/ /p/ /r/ /i/ /n/ /t/

Common exception words: house, of, the, I, a, by, to

Curriculum links (EYFS): Understanding the World: The World; (National Curriculum, Year 1): Geography: Human and physical geography

Early learning goals: Listening and attention: children listen attentively in a range of situations; Understanding: answer 'how' and 'why' questions about their experiences and in response to stories or events; Reading: read and understand simple sentences, use phonic knowledge to decode regular words and read them aloud accurately, read some common irregular words

National Curriculum learning objectives: Spoken language: listen and respond appropriately to adults and their peers; Reading/word reading: apply phonic knowledge and skills as the route to decode words, read aloud accurately books that are consistent with their developing phonic knowledge and that do not require them to use other strategies to work out words; Reading/ comprehension: understand ... books they can already read accurately and fluently ... by: drawing on what they already know or on background information and vocabulary provided by the teacher

Developing fluency

- Your child may enjoy hearing you read the book.
- You may wish to read alternate pages, encouraging your child to read with expression.

Phonic practice

- Practise reading adjacent consonants. Model sounding out the following word, saying each of the sounds quickly and clearly. Then blend the sounds together: s/p/r/i/n/t
- Ask your child to say each of the sounds in the following words. How many sounds are there in each one?
  from (4)   stop (4)   grand (4)   blocks (5)
- Now ask your child if they can read each of the words without sounding them out.